100 QUICK & EASY FAVORITE BRAND NAME RECIPES

Publications International, Ltd.
Favorite Brand Name Recipes at www.fbnr.com

Microwave Cooking: Microwave ovens vary in wattage. Use the cooking times as guidelines and check for doneness before adding more time.

Preparation/Cooking Times: Preparation times are based on the approximate amount of time required to assemble the recipe before cooking, baking, chilling or serving. These times include preparation steps such as measuring, chopping and mixing. The fact that some preparations and cooking can be done simultaneously is taken into account. Preparation of optional ingredients and serving suggestions is not included.

❧ CONTENTS ❧

SPEEDY SKILLET
SUPPERS

Harvest Apple Chicken & Rice

Prep Time: 10 minutes
Cook Time: 35 minutes

2 tablespoons margarine or butter, divided
4 boneless, skinless chicken breast halves (about 1 pound)
1 (6.0-ounce) package RICE-A-RONI® Herb Roasted Chicken Flavor
1 cup apple juice
1 medium apple, chopped (about 1 cup)
1 cup sliced mushrooms
½ cup chopped onion
¼ cup dried cranberries or raisins

1. In large skillet over medium-high heat, melt 1 tablespoon margarine. Add chicken; cook 2 minutes on each side or until browned. Remove from skillet; set aside.

2. In same skillet over medium heat, sauté rice-pasta mix with remaining 1 tablespoon margarine until pasta is golden brown.

3. Slowly stir in 1¼ cups water, apple juice, apple, mushrooms, onion, cranberries and Special Seasonings; bring to a boil. Place chicken over rice. Reduce heat to medium-low. Cover; simmer 15 to 20 minutes or until chicken is no longer pink inside and rice is tender. Let stand 5 minutes before serving. *Makes 4 servings*

Tip: No need to peel the apple—it adds extra color and texture.

Peppers Penne

8 ounces BARILLA® Penne or Mostaccioli
1 tablespoon olive or vegetable oil
1 each red, green and yellow bell pepper, cut into long, thin strips
1 jar (26 ounces) BARILLA® Marinara Pasta Sauce
2 tablespoons grated Parmesan cheese

1. Cook penne according to package directions; drain.

2. Meanwhile, heat olive oil in large skillet. Add bell peppers; cook and stir over high heat 1 minute. Reduce heat; stir in pasta sauce. Cook 5 minutes over medium heat, stirring frequently.

3. Pour pepper mixture over hot drained penne. Sprinkle with cheese.
Makes 6 to 8 servings

Variation: Add 1 cup coarsely chopped pepperoni with the pasta sauce.

15-Minute Beef Stew

Prep Time: 5 minutes
Cook Time: 15 minutes

1 tablespoon olive or vegetable oil
1 pound boneless sirloin steak, cut into 1-inch cubes
1 envelope LIPTON® RECIPE SECRETS® Onion Soup Mix*
1 cup water
2 tablespoons tomato paste
1 can (14½ ounces) new potatoes, drained and cut into chunks
1 package (10 ounces) frozen peas and carrots, thawed

*Also terrific with LIPTON® RECIPE SECRETS® Onion Mushroom, Beefy Onion or Beefy Mushroom Soup Mix.

1. In 12-inch nonstick skillet, heat oil over medium-high heat and brown steak.

2. Stir in remaining ingredients. Bring to a boil over high heat.

3. Reduce heat to low and simmer uncovered 10 minutes or until steak is tender. *Makes 4 servings*

Peppers Penne

Chicken Enchilada Skillet Casserole

Prep Time: 5 minutes
Cook Time: 10 minutes

1 bag (16 ounces) BIRDS EYE® frozen Farm Fresh Mixtures Broccoli, Corn & Red Peppers
1 package (1¼ ounces) taco seasoning mix
1 can (16 ounces) diced tomatoes, undrained
3 cups shredded cooked chicken
1 cup shredded Monterey Jack cheese
8 ounces tortilla chips

• In large skillet, combine vegetables, seasoning mix, tomatoes and chicken; bring to a boil over medium-high heat.

• Cover; cook 4 minutes or until vegetables are cooked and mixture is heated through.

• Sprinkle with cheese; cover and cook 2 minutes more or until cheese is melted.

• Serve with chips.

Makes 4 servings

Skillet Italiano

1 pound ground beef
½ medium onion, chopped
1 package (1.5 ounces) LAWRY'S® Original-Style Spaghetti Sauce Spices & Seasonings
1 can (14½ ounces) whole tomatoes, cut up, undrained
1 package (10 ounces) frozen Italian-cut green beans, thawed
LAWRY'S® Seasoned Salt to taste
1 cup (4 ounces) shredded cheddar cheese

In large skillet, cook ground beef and onion until beef is browned and crumbly; drain fat. Add Original-Style Spaghetti Sauce Spices & Seasonings, tomatoes and beans; mix well. Bring to a boil over medium-high heat; reduce heat to low, cover and simmer 20 minutes. Add Seasoned Salt to taste. Top with cheese; cover and heat until cheese melts.

Makes 4 to 6 servings

Serving Suggestion: Serve with warm bread and a tossed fruit salad.

Chicken Enchilada Skillet Casserole

Smoked Sausage and Noodle Skillet

1 tablespoon vegetable oil
1 pound **HILLSHIRE FARM®** **Smoked Sausage, cut into ¼-inch slices**
1 onion, chopped
3 cups frozen broccoli, cauliflower and carrots mixture
4 ounces uncooked medium-size noodles or curly noodles
1 can (10¾ ounces) reduced-sodium condensed cream of celery soup, undiluted
1 cup reduced-sodium chicken broth
½ teaspoon dried marjoram leaves
¼ teaspoon black pepper

Heat oil in medium skillet over medium heat. Cook and stir Smoked Sausage and onion 3 to 4 minutes. Stir in frozen vegetables, noodles, soup, chicken broth, ¾ cup water, marjoram and pepper. Bring to a boil; reduce heat. Simmer, covered, 12 to 15 minutes or until noodles are tender, stirring occasionally.

Makes 4 servings

Mediterranean Skillet Dinner

Prep Time: 10 minutes
Cook Time: 25 minutes

1½ pounds ground beef
1 medium onion, chopped
1 large eggplant (about 2 pounds), unpeeled and cut into ½-inch cubes
¼ teaspoon dried rosemary leaves, crushed
1 jar (26 to 28 ounces) **RAGÚ® Hearty Robusto!™ Pasta Sauce**
1 cup shredded mozzarella cheese (about 4 ounces)

1. In 12-inch skillet, cook ground beef and onion over medium-high heat; drain.

2. Add eggplant and rosemary and cook, stirring frequently, 10 minutes or until eggplant is tender. Season, if desired, with salt and ground black pepper. Stir in Ragú Pasta Sauce and simmer over medium-low heat, stirring occasionally, 5 minutes.

3. Sprinkle with cheese. Reduce heat to low and simmer, covered, 1 minute or until cheese is melted. Serve, if desired, over hot cooked pasta.

Makes 4 servings

Tip: Substitute an equal amount of zucchini, squash or mixed vegetables for eggplant.

Smoked Sausage and Noodle Skillet

Noodles Stroganoff

- 1 package (12 ounces) BARILLA® Wide or Extra Wide Egg Noodles
- 2 tablespoons butter or margarine
- 2 packages (8 ounces each) sliced mushrooms
- 1 medium onion, chopped
- 1 clove garlic, minced *or* ½ teaspoon bottled minced garlic
- 1½ teaspoons salt
- ½ teaspoon pepper
- 1 pound ground beef
- 1 jar (12 ounces) beef gravy
- 1 container (8 ounces) sour cream
- ⅛ teaspoon paprika

1. Cook noodles according to package directions; drain.

2. Meanwhile, melt butter in large skillet. Add mushrooms, onion, garlic, salt and pepper. Cook over medium heat, stirring occasionally, until mushrooms are lightly browned. Add ground beef and cook until no longer pink, stirring to break up meat.

3. Add gravy and heat to boiling. Remove from heat; stir in sour cream. Serve beef mixture over noodles; sprinkle with paprika.

Makes 8 to 10 servings

15 Minute Chicken Parmesan Risotto

- 1 tablespoon vegetable oil
- 1 pound boneless skinless chicken breasts, cut into small pieces
- 1 large tomato (optional)
- 1 can (10¾ ounces) cream of chicken soup
- 1⅔ cups milk
- ½ cup (2 ounces) KRAFT® 100% Grated Parmesan Cheese
- ½ teaspoon Italian seasoning (optional)
- 2 cups MINUTE® White Rice, uncooked

HEAT oil in skillet. Add chicken; cook until lightly browned. While chicken is cooking, chop tomato.

ADD soup, milk, Parmesan cheese and seasoning; stir. Heat to a boil.

STIR in rice and tomato; cover. Cook on low heat 5 minutes or until cooked through. Stir.   *Makes 4 servings*

Note: Substitute any cream soup for cream of chicken soup.

Savory Chicken with Mushrooms & Spinach

2 tablespoons margarine or butter
1 pound boneless skinless chicken breast halves, pounded thin
1½ cups sliced fresh or canned mushrooms
1 package (10 ounces) fresh spinach, rinsed and drained*
1 envelope LIPTON® RECIPE SECRETS® Savory Herb with Garlic Soup Mix**
1¼ cups water

Substitution: Use 1 package (10 ounces) frozen leaf spinach, thawed and squeezed dry.

**Also terrific with LIPTON® RECIPE SECRETS® Golden Onion Soup Mix.*

1. In 12-inch skillet, heat 1 tablespoon margarine over medium-high heat and cook chicken until no longer pink; remove and keep warm.

2. In same skillet, heat remaining 1 tablespoon margarine over medium heat and cook mushrooms, stirring frequently, 2 minutes. Add spinach and cook, stirring occasionally, 3 minutes.

3. Stir in savory herb with garlic soup mix blended with water. Bring to a boil over high heat; continue boiling, stirring occasionally, 5 minutes or until sauce is thickened.

4. To serve, arrange chicken over vegetable mixture. Serve, if desired, with hot cooked rice.

Makes 4 servings

Potato & Onion Frittata

Prep Time: 5 minutes
Cook Time: 15 minutes

1 small baking potato, peeled, halved and sliced ⅛-inch thick (about ½ cup)
¼ cup chopped onion
1 clove garlic, minced
Dash ground black pepper
1 tablespoon FLEISCHMANN'S® Original Margarine
1 cup EGG BEATERS® Healthy Real Egg Product

In 8-inch nonstick skillet, over medium-high heat, sauté potato, onion, garlic and pepper in margarine until tender. Pour Egg Beaters evenly into skillet over potato mixture. Cook without stirring for 5 to 6 minutes or until cooked on bottom and almost set on top. Carefully turn frittata; cook for 1 to 2 minutes more or until done. Slide onto serving platter; cut into wedges to serve.

Makes 2 servings

Country French Chicken Skillet

Prep Time: 5 minutes
Cook Time: 16 minutes

2 tablespoons margarine or butter
1½ pounds boneless, skinless chicken breast halves
1 cup water
1 package KNORR® Recipe Classics™ Vegetable or Spring Vegetable Soup, Dip and Recipe Mix
¼ teaspoon dried dill weed (optional)
½ cup sour cream

• In large skillet, melt margarine over medium-high heat and brown chicken, turning occasionally, 5 minutes.

• Stir in water, recipe mix and dill weed. Bring to a boil over high heat. Reduce heat to low and simmer, covered, stirring occasionally, 10 minutes or until chicken is no longer pink. Remove chicken to serving·platter and keep warm.

• Remove skillet from heat; stir in sour cream. Spoon sauce over chicken and serve, if desired, with noodles.
Makes 4 to 6 servings

Sweet and Sour Pork

Prep Time: 5 minutes
Cook Time: 15 to 18 minutes

¾ pound boneless pork
1 teaspoon vegetable oil
1 bag (16 ounces) BIRDS EYE® frozen Farm Fresh Mixtures Pepper Stir Fry vegetables
1 tablespoon water
1 jar (14 ounces) sweet and sour sauce
1 can (8 ounces) pineapple chunks, drained

• Cut pork into thin strips.

• In large skillet, heat oil over medium-high heat.

• Add pork; stir-fry until pork is browned.

• Add vegetables and water; cover and cook over medium heat 5 to 7 minutes or until vegetables are crisp-tender.

• Uncover; stir in sweet and sour sauce and pineapple. Cook until heated through.   *Makes 4 servings*

Serving Suggestion: Serve over hot cooked rice.

Tip: For a quick sweet and sour sauce for chicken nuggets or egg rolls, add sugar and vinegar to taste to jarred strained apricots or peaches.

Country French Chicken Skillet

Steaks with Peppers

2 tablespoons olive or vegetable oil
1½ pounds boneless beef chuck steaks, ½ inch thick (about 4 to 5)
2 medium red, green and/or yellow bell peppers, cut into thin strips
1 clove garlic, finely chopped (optional)
1 medium tomato, coarsely chopped
1 envelope LIPTON® RECIPE SECRETS® Onion or Onion-Mushroom Soup Mix
1 cup water

In 12-inch skillet, heat oil over medium-high heat and brown steaks. Remove steaks. Add peppers and garlic to skillet; cook over medium heat 5 minutes or until peppers are crisp-tender. Stir in tomato, then onion soup mix blended with water; bring to a boil over high heat. Reduce heat to low. Return steaks to skillet and simmer uncovered, stirring sauce occasionally, 25 minutes or until steaks and vegetables are tender.

Makes about 4 servings

Menu Suggestion: Serve with steak fries or baked potatoes.

Garlic Herb Chicken and Rice Skillet

Prep Time: none
Cook Time: 25 to 30 minutes

4 TYSON® Individually Fresh Frozen® Boneless, Skinless Chicken Breasts
1¾ cups water
1 box UNCLE BEN'S® COUNTRY INN® Chicken Flavored Rice
2 cups frozen broccoli, carrots and cauliflower mixture
¼ cup garlic and herb soft spreadable cheese

COOK: CLEAN: Wash hands. In large skillet, combine chicken, water and contents of seasoning packet. Bring to a boil. Cover and reduce heat; simmer 10 minutes. Stir in rice, vegetables and cheese. Cook, covered, 10 to 15 minutes or until internal juices of chicken run clear. (Or insert instant-read meat thermometer in thickest part of chicken. Temperature should read 170°F.) Remove from heat; let stand 5 minutes or until liquid is absorbed.

SERVE: Dish out chicken to individual plates and serve while hot.

CHILL: Refrigerate leftovers immediately.
Makes 4 servings

Chicken and Broccoli Skillet

Prep Time: 10 minutes
Cook Time: 15 minutes

1 tablespoon olive or vegetable oil
4 boneless, skinless chicken breast halves (about 1¼ pounds)
1 cup water
1 cup milk
1 tablespoon Dijon mustard
1 package KNORR® Recipe Classics™ Leek Soup, Dip and Recipe Mix
1 package (10 ounces) frozen broccoli florets (2 cups)
1 cup shredded Cheddar or Swiss cheese (about 4 ounces)
¼ cup chopped roasted red peppers (optional)
Hot cooked rice

• In large skillet, heat oil over medium-high heat and brown chicken. Remove chicken and set aside.

• In same skillet, stir in water, milk, mustard and recipe mix. Stirring frequently, bring to a boil. Add broccoli; return chicken to skillet. Reduce heat to low and simmer covered 8 minutes or until chicken is no longer pink.

• Add cheese and roasted red peppers. Stir until cheese is melted. Serve over hot rice.

Makes 4 servings

Chuckwagon BBQ Rice Round-Up

Prep Time: 5 minutes
Cook Time: 25 minutes

1 pound lean ground beef
1 (6.8-ounce) package RICE-A-RONI® Beef Flavor
2 tablespoons margarine or butter
2 cups frozen corn
½ cup prepared barbecue sauce
½ cup (2 ounces) shredded Cheddar cheese

1. In large skillet over medium-high heat, brown ground beef until well cooked. Remove from skillet; drain. Set aside.

2. In same skillet over medium heat, sauté rice-vermicelli mix with margarine until vermicelli is golden brown.

3. Slowly stir in 2½ cups water, corn and Special Seasonings; bring to a boil. Reduce heat to low. Cover; simmer 15 to 20 minutes or until rice is tender.

4. Stir in barbecue sauce and ground beef. Sprinkle with cheese. Cover; let stand 3 to 5 minutes or until cheese is melted. *Makes 4 servings*

Tip: Salsa can be substituted for barbecue sauce.

Chicken Rustigo

Prep Time: 10 minutes
Cook Time: 21 minutes

4 boneless skinless chicken breast halves
1 package (10 ounces) fresh mushrooms, sliced
¾ cup chicken broth
¼ cup dry red wine or water
3 tablespoons *French's*® Hearty Deli Brown Mustard
2 plum tomatoes, coarsely chopped
1 can (14 ounces) artichoke hearts, drained and quartered
2 teaspoons cornstarch

1. Season chicken with salt and pepper. Heat *1 tablespoon oil* in large nonstick skillet over medium-high heat. Cook chicken 5 minutes or until browned on both sides. Remove and set aside.

2. Heat *1 tablespoon oil* in same skillet over medium-high heat until hot. Add mushrooms. Cook and stir 5 minutes or until mushrooms are tender. Stir in broth, wine and mustard. Return chicken to skillet. Add tomatoes and artichoke hearts. Heat to boiling. Reduce heat to medium-low. Cook, covered, 10 minutes or until chicken is no longer pink in center.

3. Combine cornstarch and *1 tablespoon cold water* in small bowl. Stir into skillet. Heat to boiling. Cook, stirring, over high heat about 1 minute or until sauce thickens. Serve with hot cooked orzo pasta, if desired.
Makes 4 servings

Skillet Sausage with Potatoes and Rosemary

1 tablespoon vegetable oil
3 cups diced red skin potatoes
1 cup diced onion
1 pound BOB EVANS® Original Recipe Roll Sausage
½ teaspoon dried rosemary
¼ teaspoon rubbed sage
Salt and black pepper to taste
2 tablespoons chopped fresh parsley

Heat oil in large skillet over medium-high heat 1 minute. Add potatoes; cook 5 to 10 minutes or until slightly brown, stirring occasionally. Add onion; cook until tender. Add crumbled sausage; cook until browned. Add rosemary, sage, salt and pepper; cook and stir until well blended. Transfer to serving platter and garnish with parsley. Refrigerate leftovers. *Makes 4 to 6 servings*

∽ QUICK TIP ∽

Red-skinned potatoes have thin skins and waxy flesh; they are better for boiling than russet potatoes, but they can also be fried or roasted.

FAST-FIXIN'
CASSEROLES

Harvest Pot Roast with Sweet Potatoes

1 envelope LIPTON® RECIPE
    SECRETS® Onion Soup Mix
1½ cups water
¼ cup soy sauce
2 tablespoons firmly packed
    dark brown sugar
1 teaspoon ground ginger
    (optional)
1 (3- to 3½-pound) boneless pot
    roast (rump, chuck or round)
4 large sweet potatoes, peeled,
    if desired, and cut into large
    chunks
3 tablespoons water
2 tablespoons all-purpose flour

1. Preheat oven to 325°F. In Dutch oven or 5-quart heavy ovenproof saucepot, combine soup mix, water, soy sauce, brown sugar and ginger; add roast.

2. Cover and bake 1 hour 45 minutes.

3. Add potatoes and bake covered an additional 45 minutes or until beef and potatoes are tender.

4. Remove roast and potatoes to serving platter and keep warm; reserve juices.

5. In small cup, with wire whisk, blend water and flour. In Dutch oven, add flour mixture to reserved juices. Bring to a boil over high heat. Boil, stirring occasionally, 2 minutes. Serve with roast and potatoes.

Makes 6 servings

Penne, Sausage & Ham Casserole

**1 pound HILLSHIRE FARM®
   Smoked Sausage, cut into
   ½-inch slices**
**4 ounces HILLSHIRE FARM® Ham,
   cubed**
2 cups milk
2 tablespoons all-purpose flour
**8 ounces uncooked penne
   pasta, cooked and drained**
**2½ cups (10 ounces) shredded
   mozzarella cheese**
⅓ cup grated Parmesan cheese
**1 jar (16 ounces) prepared
   pasta sauce**
⅓ cup bread crumbs

Preheat oven to 350°F.

Lightly brown Smoked Sausage and Ham in large skillet over medium heat. Stir in milk and flour; bring to a boil, stirring constantly. Stir in pasta and cheeses. Pour sausage mixture into small casserole; pour pasta sauce over top. Bake, covered, 25 minutes. Uncover and sprinkle with bread crumbs; place under broiler to brown topping. *Makes 4 servings*

Chicken Caesar Tetrazzini

8 ounces uncooked spaghetti
**2 cups shredded or cubed
   cooked chicken**
1 cup chicken broth
**1 cup HIDDEN VALLEY® Caesar
   Dressing**
**1 jar (4½ ounces) sliced
   mushrooms, drained**
½ cup grated Parmesan cheese
2 tablespoons dry bread crumbs

Cook spaghetti according to package directions. Drain and combine with chicken, broth, dressing and mushrooms in a large mixing bowl. Place mixture in a 2-quart casserole. Mix together cheese and bread crumbs; sprinkle over spaghetti mixture. Bake at 350°F. for 25 minutes or until casserole is hot and bubbly.
Makes 4 servings

∽ QUICK TIP ∽

Pasta that is to be baked in a casserole should be slightly undercooked or it will be too soft after baking.

Penne, Sausage & Ham Casserole

1-2-3 Cheddar Broccoli Casserole

Prep Time: 5 minutes
Cook Time: 20 minutes

1 jar (16 ounces) RAGÚ® Cheese
 Creations!® Double Cheddar
 Sauce
2 boxes (10 ounces each) frozen
 broccoli florets, thawed
¼ cup plain or Italian seasoned
 dry bread crumbs
1 tablespoon margarine or
 butter, melted

1. Preheat oven to 350°F. In 1½-quart casserole, combine Ragú Cheese Creations! Sauce and broccoli.

2. Evenly top with bread crumbs combined with margarine.

3. Bake uncovered 20 minutes or until bread crumbs are golden and broccoli is tender.

Makes 6 servings

Tip: Substitute your favorite frozen vegetables for broccoli florets.

Main-Dish Pie

Prep Time: 10 minutes
Cook Time: 20 to 25 minutes

1 package (8 rolls) refrigerated
 crescent rolls
1 pound lean ground beef
1 medium onion, chopped
1 can (12 ounces) beef or
 mushroom gravy
1 box (10 ounces) BIRDS EYE®
 frozen Green Peas, thawed
½ cup shredded Swiss cheese
6 slices tomato

• Preheat oven to 350°F.

• Unroll dough and separate rolls. Spread to cover bottom of ungreased 9-inch pie pan. Press together to form lower crust. Bake 10 minutes.

• Meanwhile, in large skillet, brown beef and onion; drain excess fat.

• Stir in gravy and peas; cook until heated through.

• Pour mixture into partially baked crust. Sprinkle with cheese.

• Bake 10 to 15 minutes or until crust is brown and cheese is melted.

• Arrange tomato slices over pie; bake 2 minutes more.

Makes 6 servings

Florentine Strata

8 ounces **BARILLA® Spaghetti or Linguine**

1 jar (26 ounces) **BARILLA® Roasted Garlic and Onion Pasta Sauce, divided**

1 package (12 ounces) frozen spinach soufflé, thawed

2 cups (8 ounces) shredded mozzarella cheese, divided

¼ cup (1 ounce) grated Parmesan cheese, divided

1. Cook spaghetti according to package directions until partially done but still firm, 5 to 8 minutes. Drain.

2. Meanwhile, coat microwave-safe 13×9×2-inch baking dish with nonstick cooking spray. Pour 1½ cups pasta sauce into baking dish; top with half of drained spaghetti, half of spinach soufflé, 1 cup mozzarella cheese and 2 tablespoons Parmesan. Repeat layers of spaghetti, pasta sauce and cheeses.

3. Cover with plastic wrap and microwave on HIGH, turning every 4 minutes, until strata is bubbly and cheese is melted, 8 to 10 minutes. Let stand 3 minutes before serving.

Makes 8 servings

Tip: When preparing pasta that will be used in a casserole, it's important to reduce the suggested cooking time on the package by about one third. The pasta will continue to cook and absorb liquid while the casserole is cooking.

Oven-Baked Stew

Prep Time: 15 minutes
Cook Time: 2 hours

2 pounds boneless beef chuck or round steak, cut into 1-inch cubes

¼ cup all-purpose flour

1⅓ cups sliced carrots

1 can (14 to 16 ounces) whole peeled tomatoes, undrained and chopped

1 envelope **LIPTON® RECIPE SECRETS® Onion Soup Mix***

½ cup dry red wine or water

1 cup fresh or canned sliced mushrooms

1 package (8 ounces) medium or broad egg noodles, cooked and drained

*Also terrific with LIPTON® RECIPE SECRETS® Beefy Onion, Onion Mushroom or Beefy Mushroom Soup Mix.

1. Preheat oven to 425°F. In 2½-quart shallow casserole, toss beef with flour, then bake uncovered 20 minutes, stirring once.

2. Reduce heat to 350°F. Stir in carrots, tomatoes, soup mix and wine.

3. Bake covered 1½ hours or until beef is tender. Stir in mushrooms and bake covered an additional 10 minutes. Serve over hot noodles.

Makes 8 servings

Slow Cooker Method: Toss beef with flour and place in slow cooker. Add carrots, tomatoes, soup mix and wine. Cover. Cook on LOW 8 hours. Add mushrooms; cover and cook 30 minutes or until beef is tender. Serve over hot noodles.

Golden Grits Casserole

1 cup quick cooking grits
2 cups (8 ounces) reduced fat shredded cheddar cheese
½ cup margarine, melted
½ teaspoon LAWRY'S® Seasoned Salt
⅛ to ¼ teaspoon cayenne pepper
2 eggs, beaten
1 tablespoon chopped parsley

Prepare grits as directed on package. Add 1 cup cheese, margarine, Seasoned Salt and cayenne to cooked grits; mix well. Add small amount of grits mixture to eggs; then add egg mixture back to grits. Stir until cheese is melted and margarine is blended. Pour into lightly greased 2-quart glass casserole. Top with remaining cheese. Bake at 350°F. 1 hour. Let stand 15 minutes before serving.　　*Makes 6 servings*

Serving Suggestion: Sprinkle with parsley. Serve with roasted beef or chicken.

Microwave: Prepare grits as directed above. Pour into 2-quart glass casserole. Microwave on MEDIUM 13 to 15 minutes, or until heated through and set. Sprinkle with remaining cheese. Cook on MEDIUM 1 to 2 minutes until cheese is melted. Continue as directed above. Let stand 15 minutes before serving.

Baked Cabbage with Smoked Sausage

1 head cabbage
¼ pound HILLSHIRE FARM® Bacon, sliced
Salt and black pepper to taste
1 onion, finely chopped
½ cup white wine
½ cup beef broth
1 pound HILLSHIRE FARM® Smoked Sausage, cut into ¼-inch slices

Preheat oven to 350°F.

Clean and quarter cabbage; soak in salted water. Line large casserole with Bacon; add cabbage. Season cabbage with salt and pepper; sprinkle with onion. Pour wine and beef broth over cabbage; top with Smoked Sausage. Bake, covered, 1 hour or until cooked through.
Makes 4 servings

Pork Chops and Yams

4 pork chops (½ inch thick)
2 tablespoons oil
2 (16-ounce) cans yams or sweet potatoes, drained
¾ cup SMUCKER'S® Sweet Orange Marmalade or Apricot Preserves
½ large green bell pepper, cut into strips
2 tablespoons minced onion

Brown pork chops in oil over medium heat.

Place yams in 1½-quart casserole. Stir in marmalade, bell pepper and onion. Layer pork chops over yam mixture. Cover and bake at 350°F for 30 minutes or until pork chops are tender.　　*Makes 4 servings*

Chicken Parmesan Noodle Bake

Prep & Cook Time: 35 minutes

1 package (12 ounces) extra-wide noodles
4 boneless, skinless chicken breast halves
1/4 teaspoon rosemary, crushed
2 cans (14 1/2 ounces each) DEL MONTE® Diced Tomatoes with Basil, Garlic & Oregano
1/2 cup (2 ounces) shredded mozzarella cheese
1/4 cup (1 ounce) grated Parmesan cheese

1. Preheat oven to 450°F.

2. Cook noodles according to package directions; drain.

3. Meanwhile, sprinkle chicken with rosemary; season with salt and pepper, if desired. Arrange chicken in 13×9-inch baking dish. Bake, uncovered, 20 minutes or until chicken is no longer pink in center. Drain; remove chicken from dish.

4. Drain tomatoes, reserving liquid. In large bowl, toss reserved liquid with noodles; place in baking dish. Top with chicken and tomatoes; sprinkle with cheeses.

5. Bake 10 minutes or until heated through. Sprinkle with additional Parmesan cheese and garnish, if desired. *Makes 4 servings*

Carolina Baked Beans & Pork Chops

Prep Time: 10 minutes
Cook Time: 30 minutes

2 cans (16 ounces each) pork and beans
1/2 cup chopped onion
1/2 cup chopped green bell pepper
1/4 cup *French's® Classic Yellow®* Mustard
1/4 cup packed light brown sugar
2 tablespoons *French's®* Worcestershire Sauce
1 tablespoon *Frank's® RedHot®* Cayenne Pepper Sauce
6 boneless pork chops (1 inch thick)

1. Preheat oven to 400°F. Combine all ingredients *except pork chops* in 3-quart shallow baking dish; mix well. Arrange chops on top, turning once to coat with sauce.

2. Bake, uncovered, 30 to 35 minutes or until pork is no longer pink in center. Stir beans around chops once during baking. Serve with green beans or mashed potatoes, if desired. *Makes 6 servings*

Turkey and Stuffing Bake

1 jar (4½ ounces) sliced mushrooms
¼ cup butter or margarine
½ cup diced celery
½ cup chopped onion
1¼ cups **HIDDEN VALLEY**® Original Ranch® Dressing, divided
⅔ cup water
3 cups seasoned stuffing mix
⅓ cup sweetened dried cranberries
3 cups coarsely shredded cooked turkey (about 1 pound)

Drain mushrooms, reserving liquid; set aside. Melt butter over medium-high heat in a large skillet. Add celery and onion; sauté for 4 minutes or until soft. Remove from heat and stir in ½ cup dressing, water and reserved mushroom liquid. Stir in stuffing mix and cranberries until thoroughly moistened. Combine turkey, mushrooms and remaining ¾ cup dressing in a separate bowl; spread evenly in a greased 8-inch baking dish. Top with stuffing mixture. Bake at 350°F. for 40 minutes or until bubbly and brown. *Makes 4 to 6 servings*

Rigatoni Con Ricotta

1 package (16 ounces) **BARILLA**® Rigatoni
2 eggs
1 container (15 ounces) ricotta cheese
¾ cup (3 ounces) grated Parmesan cheese
1 tablespoon dried parsley
2 jars (26 ounces each) **BARILLA**® Lasagna & Casserole Sauce or Marinara Pasta Sauce, divided
3 cups (12 ounces) shredded mozzarella cheese, divided

1. Preheat oven to 375°F. Spray 13×9×2-inch baking pan with nonstick cooking spray. Cook rigatoni according to package directions; drain.

2. Beat eggs in small bowl. Stir in ricotta, Parmesan and parsley.

3. To assemble casserole, spread 2 cups lasagna sauce to cover bottom of pan. Place half of cooked rigatoni over sauce; top with half of ricotta mixture, dropped by spoonfuls. Layer with 1 cup mozzarella, 2 cups lasagna sauce, remaining rigatoni and ricotta mixture. Top with 1 cup mozzarella, remaining lasagna sauce and remaining 1 cup mozzarella.

4. Cover with foil and bake 60 to 70 minutes or until bubbly. Uncover and continue cooking about 5 minutes or until cheese is melted. Let stand 15 minutes before serving.
Makes 12 servings

Turkey and Stuffing Bake

Chili Cornbread Casserole

Prep Time: 10 minutes
Cook Time: 20 minutes

1 pound ground beef
1 medium onion, chopped
1 jar (16 ounces) RAGÚ® Cheese Creations!® Double Cheddar Sauce
1 can (19 ounces) red kidney beans, rinsed and drained
1 can (8¾ ounces) whole kernel corn, drained
2 to 3 teaspoons chili powder
1 package (12 ounces) cornbread mix

1. Preheat oven to 400°F. In 12-inch skillet, brown ground beef and onion over medium-high heat; drain. Stir in Ragú Cheese Creations! Sauce, beans, corn and chili powder.

2. Meanwhile, prepare cornbread mix according to package directions. Do not bake.

3. In ungreased 2-quart baking dish, spread ground beef mixture. Top with cornbread mixture. Bake uncovered 20 minutes or until toothpick inserted in center of cornbread comes out clean and top is golden.

Makes 6 servings

One-Dish Chicken Bake

Prep Time: 10 minutes
Bake Time: 35 minutes

1 package (6 ounces) STOVE TOP® Stuffing Mix for Chicken
4 boneless skinless chicken breast halves (about 1¼ pounds)
1 can (10¾ ounces) condensed cream of mushroom soup
⅓ cup BREAKSTONE® or KNUDSEN® Sour Cream or milk

1. STIR stuffing crumbs, contents of vegetable/seasoning packet, 1½ cups hot water and ¼ cup margarine, cut-up, just until moistened; set aside.

2. PLACE chicken in 12×8-inch baking dish. Mix soup and sour cream; pour over chicken. Top with stuffing.

3. BAKE at 375°F for 35 minutes or until chicken is cooked through.

Makes 4 servings

❧ QUICK TIP ❧

Thoroughly wash cutting surfaces, utensils and your hands with hot soapy water after handling raw chicken. This eliminates the risk of contaminating other foods with salmonella bacteria that is often present in raw chicken. Salmonella is killed during cooking.

Zucchini Pasta Bake

Prep and Cook Time: *33 minutes*

1½ cups uncooked pasta tubes
½ pound ground beef
½ cup chopped onion
1 clove garlic, minced
  Salt and pepper
1 can (14½ ounces) DEL MONTE®
  Zucchini with Italian-Style
  Tomato Sauce
1 teaspoon dried basil, crushed
1 cup (4 ounces) shredded
  Monterey Jack cheese

1. Cook pasta according to package directions; drain.

2. Cook beef with onion and garlic in large skillet; drain. Season with salt and pepper.

3. Stir in zucchini with tomato sauce and basil. Place pasta in 8-inch square baking dish. Top with meat mixture.

4. Bake at 350°F for 15 minutes. Top with cheese. Bake 3 minutes or until cheese is melted.
Makes 4 servings

Weekend Brunch Casserole

1 pound BOB EVANS® Original
  Recipe Roll Sausage
1 (8-ounce) can refrigerated
  crescent dinner rolls
2 cups (8 ounces) shredded
  mozzarella cheese
4 eggs, beaten
¾ cup milk
¼ teaspoon salt
⅛ teaspoon black pepper

Preheat oven to 425°F. Crumble sausage into medium skillet. Cook over medium heat until browned, stirring occasionally. Drain off any drippings. Line bottom of greased 13×9-inch baking dish with crescent roll dough, firmly pressing perforations to seal. Sprinkle with sausage and cheese. Combine remaining ingredients in medium bowl until blended; pour over sausage. Bake 15 minutes or until set. Let stand 5 minutes before cutting into squares; serve hot. Refrigerate leftovers.
Makes 6 to 8 servings

Serving Suggestion: Serve with fresh fruit or sliced tomatoes.

SLOW COOKER

MAGIC

Barbara's Pork Chop Dinner

- 1 tablespoon butter
- 1 tablespoon olive oil
- 6 bone-in pork loin chops
- 1 can (10¾ ounces) condensed cream of chicken soup, undiluted
- 1 can (4 ounces) mushrooms, drained and chopped
- ¼ cup Dijon mustard
- ¼ cup chicken broth
- 2 cloves garlic, minced
- ½ teaspoon salt
- ½ teaspoon dried basil leaves
- ¼ teaspoon black pepper
- 6 red potatoes, unpeeled, cut into thin slices
- 1 onion, sliced
  Chopped fresh parsley

Slow Cooker Directions

Heat butter and oil in large skillet. Brown pork chops on both sides. Set aside.

Combine soup, mushrooms, mustard, chicken broth, garlic, salt, basil and pepper in slow cooker. Add potatoes and onion, stirring to coat. Place pork chops on top of potato mixture. Cover and cook on LOW 8 to 10 hours or on HIGH 4 to 5 hours. Sprinkle with parsley. *Makes 6 servings*

Barbara's Pork Chop Dinner

Chicken Sausage Pilaf

1 tablespoon vegetable oil
1 pound chicken or turkey
   sausage, casing removed
1 cup uncooked rice and pasta
   mix
4 cups chicken broth
2 ribs celery, diced
¼ cup slivered almonds
   Salt and black pepper to taste

Slow Cooker Directions
Heat oil in large skillet; add sausage.
Break up sausage with back of spoon
while cooking; cook until browned,
about 5 minutes. Add rice-pasta
mix to skillet. Cook 1 minute. Place
mixture in slow cooker. Add remaining
ingredients to slow cooker; stir well.
Cover and cook on LOW 7 to 10 hours
or on HIGH 3 to 4 hours or until rice is
tender. *Makes 4 servings*

Hearty Chili Mac

1 pound lean ground beef
1 can (14½ ounces) diced
   tomatoes, drained
1 cup chopped onion
1 clove garlic, minced
½ teaspoon salt
½ teaspoon ground cumin
½ teaspoon dried oregano
   leaves
¼ teaspoon black pepper
¼ teaspoon red pepper flakes
1 tablespoon chili powder
2 cups cooked macaroni

Crumble ground beef into slow
cooker. Add remaining ingredients,
except macaroni, to slow cooker.
Cover and cook on LOW 4 hours. Stir
in cooked macaroni. Cover and cook
on LOW 1 hour. *Makes 4 servings*

Ham and Potato Casserole

1½ pounds red potatoes, peeled
   and sliced
8 ounces thinly sliced ham
2 poblano chili peppers, cut
   into thin strips
2 tablespoons olive oil
1 tablespoon dried oregano
   leaves
¼ teaspoon salt
1 cup (4 ounces) shredded
   Monterey Jack cheese with
   or without hot peppers
2 tablespoons finely chopped
   cilantro leaves

1. Combine all ingredients, except
cheese and cilantro, in slow cooker;
mix well. Cover and cook on LOW
7 hours or on HIGH 4 hours.

2. Transfer potato mixture to serving
dish and sprinkle with cheese and
cilantro. Let stand 3 minutes or until
cheese melts.
Makes 6 to 7 servings

∽ QUICK TIP ∽

Poblano chili peppers are dark
green, 4 to 5 inches long, 2 to 3
inches wide, and taper from top to
bottom in a triangular shape. They
are found in Mexican markets and
many supermarkets.

Chicken Sausage Pilaf

Asparagus and Cheese Side Dish

1½ pounds fresh asparagus, trimmed
2 cups crushed saltine crackers
1 can (10¾ ounces) condensed cream of asparagus soup, undiluted
1 can (10¾ ounces) condensed cream of chicken soup, undiluted
¼ pound American cheese, cut into cubes
⅔ cup slivered almonds
1 egg

Slow Cooker Directions
Combine all ingredients in large bowl; stir well. Pour into slow cooker. Cover and cook on HIGH 3 to 3½ hours.

Makes 4 to 6 servings

Sweet-Spiced Sweet Potatoes

2 pounds sweet potatoes, peeled and cut into ½-inch pieces
¼ cup dark brown sugar, packed
1 teaspoon ground cinnamon
½ teaspoon ground nutmeg
⅛ teaspoon salt
2 tablespoons butter, cut into ⅛-inch pieces
1 teaspoon vanilla extract

Combine all ingredients, except butter and vanilla, in slow cooker; mix well. Cover and cook on LOW 7 hours or cook on HIGH 4 hours. Add butter and vanilla; stir to blend.

Makes 4 servings

Deviled Beef Short Rib Stew

Prep Time: 20 minutes
Cook Time: 5 minutes

4 pounds beef short ribs, trimmed
2 pounds small red potatoes, scrubbed and scored
8 carrots, peeled and cut into chunks
2 onions, cut into thick wedges
1 bottle (12 ounces) beer or non-alcoholic malt beverage
8 tablespoons *French's®* Hearty Deli Brown Mustard, divided
3 tablespoons *French's®* Worcestershire Sauce, divided
2 tablespoons cornstarch

Slow Cooker Directions
1. Broil ribs 6 inches from heat on rack in broiler pan 10 minutes or until well-browned, turning once. Place vegetables in bottom of slow cooker. Place ribs on top of vegetables.

2. Combine beer, *6 tablespoons* mustard and *2 tablespoons* Worcestershire in medium bowl. Pour into slow cooker. Cover and cook on HIGH 5 hours* or until meat is tender.

3. Transfer meat and vegetables to platter; keep warm. Strain fat from broth; pour into saucepan. Combine cornstarch with *2 tablespoons cold water* in small bowl. Stir into broth with remaining *2 tablespoons* mustard and *1 tablespoon* Worcestershire. Heat to boiling. Reduce heat to medium-low. Cook 1 to 2 minutes or until thickened, stirring often. Pass gravy with meat and vegetables. Serve meat with additional mustard.

Makes 6 servings (with 3 cups gravy)

*Or cook 10 hours on low-heat setting.

Asparagus and Cheese Side Dish

Brunswick Stew

1 package (about 2 pounds)
   PERDUE® Fresh Chicken
   Thighs
2 cans (14½ ounces each)
   chicken broth
3 potatoes, peeled and diced
   into ½-inch pieces (3 cups)
1 can (14½ ounces) Cajun- or
   Mexican-style tomatoes
1 package (10 ounces) frozen
   succotash, partially thawed
   Salt and ground black pepper
   to taste
   Hot pepper sauce to taste

Slow Cooker Directions

In slow cooker, combine chicken, chicken broth and potatoes. Cover and cook on low heat 2½ to 3 hours, until chicken is cooked through. Add tomatoes, succotash, salt and pepper. Turn heat to high; cover and cook 1 hour. Season to taste with salt, pepper and hot pepper sauce. Serve in soup bowls.

Makes 4 to 6 servings

Note: This recipe can also be cooked in a Dutch oven on top of the stove over medium-low heat for about 1 hour. For added flavor, stir in ½ cup diced PERDUE® Turkey Ham.

QUICK TIP

Using reduced-sodium chicken broth in recipes allows you to adjust the seasoning to your taste.

Beef and Vegetables in Rich Burgundy Sauce

1 package (8 ounces) sliced
   mushrooms
1 package (8 ounces) baby
   carrots
1 medium green bell pepper, cut
   into thin strips
1 boneless chuck roast
   (2½ pounds)
1 can (10½ ounces) golden
   mushroom soup
¼ cup dry red wine or beef broth
1 tablespoon Worcestershire
   sauce
1 package (1 ounce) dried
   onion soup mix
¼ teaspoon black pepper
2 tablespoons water
3 tablespoons cornstarch
4 cups hot cooked noodles
   Chopped fresh parsley
   (optional)

1. Place mushrooms, carrots and bell pepper in slow cooker. Place roast on top of vegetables. Combine soup, wine, Worcestershire sauce, soup mix and black pepper in medium bowl; mix well. Pour soup mixture over roast. Cover and cook on LOW 8 to 10 hours.

2. Blend water into cornstarch in cup until smooth; set aside. Transfer roast to cutting board; cover with foil. Let stand 10 to 15 minutes before slicing.

3. Turn slow cooker to HIGH. Stir cornstarch mixture into vegetable mixture; cover and cook 10 minutes or until thickened. Serve over cooked noodles. Garnish with parsley, if desired. *Makes 6 to 8 servings*

Turkey Mushroom Stew

- 1 **pound turkey cutlets, cut into 4×1-inch strips**
- 1 **small onion, thinly sliced**
- 2 **tablespoons minced green onions with tops**
- ½ **pound mushrooms, sliced**
- 2 to 3 **tablespoons flour**
- 1 **cup half-and-half or milk**
- 1 **teaspoon dried tarragon leaves**
- 1 **teaspoon salt**
  Black pepper to taste
- ½ **cup frozen peas**
- ½ **cup sour cream (optional)**
  Puff pastry shells (optional)

Slow Cooker Directions

Layer turkey, onions and mushrooms in slow cooker. Cover and cook on LOW 4 hours. Remove turkey and vegetables to serving bowl. Turn slow cooker to HIGH.

Blend flour into half-and-half until smooth; pour into slow cooker. Add tarragon, salt and pepper to slow cooker. Return cooked vegetables and turkey to slow cooker. Stir in peas. Cover and cook 1 hour or until sauce has thickened and peas are heated through.

Stir in sour cream just before serving, if desired. Serve in puff pastry shells.

Makes 4 servings

BBQ Pork Sandwiches

Prep Time: 10 minutes
Cook Time: 5 hours

- 4 **pounds boneless pork loin roast, fat trimmed**
- 1 **can (14½ ounces) beef broth**
- ⅓ **cup *French's*® Worcestershire Sauce**
- ⅓ **cup *Frank's*® RedHot® Cayenne Pepper Sauce**

Sauce
- ½ **cup ketchup**
- ½ **cup molasses**
- ¼ **cup *French's*® Classic Yellow® Mustard**
- ¼ **cup *French's*® Worcestershire Sauce**
- 2 **tablespoons *Frank's*® RedHot® Cayenne Pepper Sauce**

Slow Cooker Directions

1. Place roast on bottom of slow cooker. Combine broth, *⅓ cup each* Worcestershire and *Frank's RedHot* Sauce. Pour over roast. Cover and cook on high-heat setting 5 hours* or until roast is tender.

2. Meanwhile, combine ingredients for sauce in large bowl; set aside.

3. Transfer roast to large cutting board. Discard liquid. Coarsely chop roast. Stir into reserved sauce. Spoon pork mixture on large rolls. Serve with deli potato salad, if desired.

Makes 8 to 10 servings

*Or cook 10 hours on low-heat setting.

Tip: Make additional sauce and serve on the side. Great also with barbecued ribs and chops!

Simple Coq au Vin

4 chicken legs
   Salt and black pepper
2 tablespoons olive oil
½ pound mushrooms, sliced
1 onion, sliced into rings
½ cup red wine
½ teaspoon dried basil leaves
½ teaspoon dried thyme leaves
½ teaspoon dried oregano
   leaves
   Hot cooked rice

Slow Cooker Directions

Sprinkle chicken with salt and pepper. Heat oil in large skillet; brown chicken on both sides. Transfer chicken to slow cooker. Sauté mushrooms and onion in same skillet. Add wine; stir and scrape brown bits from bottom of skillet. Add mixture to slow cooker. Sprinkle with basil, thyme and oregano. Cover and cook on LOW 8 to 10 hours or on HIGH 3 to 4 hours.

Serve chicken and sauce over rice.
Makes 4 servings

Italian Sausage and Vegetable Stew

1 pound hot or mild Italian
   sausage, cut into 1-inch
   pieces
1 package (16 ounces) frozen
   mixed vegetables (onions
   and green, red and yellow
   bell peppers)
1 can (14½ ounces) diced
   Italian-style tomatoes,
   undrained
2 medium zucchini, sliced
1 jar (4½ ounces) sliced
   mushrooms, drained
4 cloves garlic, minced
2 tablespoons Italian-style
   tomato paste

Slow Cooker Directions

Heat large skillet over high heat until hot. Add sausage, cook about 5 minutes or until browned. Pour off any drippings.

Combine sausage, frozen vegetables, tomatoes, zucchini, mushrooms and garlic in slow cooker. Cover and cook on LOW 4 to 4½ hours or until zucchini is tender. Stir in tomato paste. Cover and cook 30 mintues or until juices have thickened.
Makes 6 (1-cup) servings

Serving Suggestion: Serve with fresh hot garlic bread.

Mu Shu Turkey

1 can (16 ounces) plums,
    drained, rinsed and pitted
½ cup orange juice
¼ cup finely chopped onion
1 tablespoon minced fresh
    ginger
¼ teaspoon ground cinnamon
1 pound boneless turkey breast,
    cut into thin strips
6 (7-inch) flour tortillas
3 cups coleslaw mix

1. Place plums in blender or food processor. Cover and blend until almost smooth. Combine plums, orange juice, onion, ginger and cinnamon in slow cooker; mix well. Place turkey strips over plum mixture. Cover and cook on LOW 3 to 4 hours.

2. Remove turkey strips from slow cooker and divide evenly among the tortillas. Spoon about 2 tablespoons plum sauce over turkey. Top evenly with coleslaw mix. Fold bottom edge of tortilla over filling; fold in sides. Roll up to completely enclose filling. Repeat with remaining tortillas. Use remaining plum sauce for dipping.

Makes 6 servings

Easy Weeknight Chicken Cacciatore

Prep Time: 10 minutes
Cook Time: 40 minutes

1 tablespoon olive or vegetable
    oil
2½ pounds chicken pieces
1 package (8 ounces) fresh
    mushrooms, sliced
1 can (28 ounces) crushed
    tomatoes
1 envelope LIPTON® RECIPE
    SECRETS® Onion Soup Mix
¼ cup dry red wine
½ teaspoon dried basil

1. In 6-quart saucepot, heat oil over medium-high heat and brown chicken pieces. Add mushrooms and cook 2 minutes, stirring occasionally.

2. Stir in crushed tomatoes, soup mix, wine and basil. Bring to a boil over high heat.

3. Reduce heat to low and simmer, covered, 30 minutes or until chicken is no longer pink. Serve, if desired, over hot cooked noodles or rice.

Makes 4 servings

Slow Cooker Method: Place mushrooms then chicken pieces in slow cooker. Stir crushed tomatoes, soup mix, wine and basil together until blended. Pour over chicken and mushrooms. Cover. Cook on HIGH 4 to 6 hours or LOW 8 hours. Serve as above.

Vegetarian Chili

1 tablespoon vegetable oil
1 cup finely chopped onion
1 cup chopped red bell pepper
2 tablespoons minced jalapeño pepper
1 clove garlic, minced
1 can (28 ounces) crushed tomatoes
1 can (15 ounces) black beans, rinsed and drained
1 can (15 ounces) garbanzo beans, drained
½ cup canned corn
¼ cup tomato paste
1 teaspoon sugar
1 teaspoon ground cumin
1 teaspoon dried basil leaves
1 teaspoon chili powder
¼ teaspoon black pepper
1 cup shredded Cheddar cheese (optional)
Sour cream (optional)

1. Heat oil in large nonstick skillet over medium-high heat until hot. Add chopped onion, bell pepper, jalapeño pepper and garlic; cook and stir 5 minutes or until vegetables are tender.

2. Spoon vegetables into slow cooker. Add remaining ingredients, except cheese, to slow cooker; mix well. Cover and cook on LOW 4 to 5 hours. Garnish with cheese and sour cream, if desired. *Makes 4 servings*

Oniony Braised Short Ribs

Prep Time: 10 minutes
Cook Time: 2 hours 15 minutes

2 tablespoons olive or vegetable oil
3 pounds beef chuck short ribs
1 envelope LIPTON® RECIPE SECRETS® Onion Soup Mix
3¼ cups water
¼ cup ketchup
2 tablespoons firmly packed brown sugar
2 tablespoons sherry (optional)
½ teaspoon ground ginger
1 tablespoon all-purpose flour
¼ cup water
¼ teaspoon ground black pepper

1. In 6-quart Dutch oven or saucepot, heat oil over medium-high heat and brown short ribs in two batches. Return ribs to Dutch oven.

2. Stir in soup mix combined with 3¼ cups water, ketchup, brown sugar, sherry and ginger. Bring to a boil. Reduce heat to low; simmer, covered, 2 hours or until ribs are tender.

3. Remove ribs to serving platter and keep warm. In Dutch oven, add flour combined with ¼ cup water and pepper. Bring to a boil over high heat. Boil, stirring occasionally, 2 minutes or until thickened. Pour sauce over ribs. Serve, if desired, with crusty bread.
Makes 4 servings

Slow Cooker Method: Place short ribs in slow cooker. Combine 2½ cups water with soup mix, ketchup, brown sugar, sherry and ginger. Pour over ribs. Cover and cook on LOW 8 to 10 hours or until ribs are tender. Remove ribs to serving platter. Stir ¼ cup water with flour and black pepper into juices in slow cooker. Cover and cook on HIGH 15 minutes or until thickened. Pour over ribs.

Vegetarian Chili

PASTA PRONTO

Spaghetti with Meat and Mushroom Sauce

  1 package (16 ounces) BARILLA®
    Spaghetti or Thick Spaghetti
  1 large onion, chopped
  2 tablespoons minced garlic
  ¼ cup olive oil
  1 pound strip loin steak, cut into
    ½-inch cubes
2½ cups (6 ounces) sliced
    mushrooms
  1 cup chopped red, yellow and
    green bell peppers
  1 medium tomato, chopped
  1 jar (26 ounces) BARILLA®
    Tomato and Basil Pasta
    Sauce
  ¼ cup red wine
  1 tablespoon dried Italian
    seasoning
    Salt and pepper
    Grated Parmesan cheese

1. Cook spaghetti according to package directions; drain.

2. Meanwhile, cook onion and garlic in olive oil in Dutch oven or large pot over medium heat until onion is transparent. Add steak; cook and stir over medium-high heat 4 minutes. Add vegetables; cook and stir 4 minutes. Stir in pasta sauce, wine and Italian seasoning; heat just to boiling, stirring frequently. Add salt and pepper to taste.

3. Combine sauce with hot drained spaghetti. Cover and let stand 2 minutes before serving. Serve with cheese.   *Makes 8 to 10 servings*

Tip: To enhance flavor, substitute ¼ cup finely chopped fresh herbs for 1 tablespoon dried Italian seasoning.

Spaghetti with Meat and Mushroom Sauce

Spinach Tortellini with Roasted Red Peppers

2 packages (9 ounces each) refrigerated spinach tortellini
1 jar (7 ounces) roasted red peppers, rinsed and drained
2 tablespoons butter or olive oil
4 cloves garlic, minced
¼ cup chopped fresh basil *or* 2 teaspoons dried basil, crushed
½ cup chopped walnuts or pine nuts, toasted
1 cup HIDDEN VALLEY® Original Ranch® Dressing
Fresh basil leaves (optional)

Cook tortellini according to package directions; drain and set aside. Slice red peppers into strips; set aside. Melt butter in medium saucepan; add garlic and sauté for about 2 minutes. Stir in tortellini, red pepper strips, basil and walnuts. Stir in dressing until mixture is creamy and tortellini are coated. Garnish with basil leaves, if desired.   *Makes 4 to 6 servings*

Zesty Artichoke Pesto Sauce

Prep time: 5 minutes
Cook Time: 19 minutes

1 jar (6 ounces) marinated artichoke hearts, chopped, marinade reserved
1 cup sliced onion
1 can (14.5 ounces) CONTADINA® Recipe Ready Diced Tomatoes, undrained
1 can (6 ounces) CONTADINA® Italian Paste with Tomato Pesto
1 cup water
½ teaspoon salt
Hot cooked pasta

1. Heat reserved artichoke marinade in large saucepan over medium-high heat until warm.

2. Add onion; cook for 3 to 4 minutes or until tender. Add artichoke hearts, tomatoes and juice, tomato paste, water and salt.

3. Bring to a boil; reduce heat to low. Cook, stirring occasionally, for 10 to 15 minutes or until flavors are blended. Serve over pasta.
          Makes 6 to 8 servings

Savory Caper and Olive Sauce:
Eliminate artichoke hearts. Heat 2 tablespoons olive oil in large saucepan over medium-high heat. Add onion; cook for 3 to 4 minutes or until tender. Add tomatoes and juice, tomato paste, water, salt, ¾ cup sliced and quartered zucchini, ½ cup (2¼-ounce can) drained sliced ripe olives and 2 tablespoons capers. Proceed as above.

Spinach Tortellini with Roasted Red Peppers

Penne with Red Pepper Alfredo Sauce

Prep Time: *10 minutes*
Cook Time: *10 minutes*

- **1 jar (7.25 ounces) roasted red peppers, drained**
- **1 jar (16 ounces) RAGÚ® Cheese Creations!® Classic Alfredo Sauce**
- **8 ounces penne or ziti pasta, cooked and drained**

1. In blender or food processor, purée roasted peppers.

2. In 2-quart saucepan, heat Ragú Cheese Creations! Sauce over medium heat. Stir in puréed roasted peppers; heat through. Toss with hot pasta and garnish, if desired, with chopped fresh basil leaves.

Makes 4 servings

Santa Fe Chicken & Pasta

Prep Time: *10 minutes*
Cook Time: *43 minutes*

- **1 jar (12 ounces) mild chunky salsa**
- **1 can (10¾ ounces) condensed Cheddar cheese soup**
- **¾ cup sour cream**
- **5 cups hot cooked ziti pasta (8 ounces uncooked)**
- **1⅓ cups *French's® Taste Toppers™* French Fried Onions, divided**
- **1 package (10 ounces) fully cooked carved chicken breast (2 cups cut-up chicken)**
- **1 cup (4 ounces) cubed Monterey Jack cheese with jalapeño**

1. Preheat oven to 375°F. In large bowl, mix salsa, soup and sour cream. Stir in pasta, ⅔ cup **Taste Toppers**, chicken and cheese; mix well. Spoon into 3-quart casserole.

2. Cover; bake 40 minutes or until hot and bubbly. Stir.

3. Sprinkle with remaining ⅔ cup **Taste Toppers**. Bake 3 minutes or until **Taste Toppers** are golden.

Makes 8 servings

Penne with Red Pepper Alfredo Sauce

Chicken Dijon with Spinach

Prep Time: 15 minutes
Cook Time: about 10 minutes

1 pound boneless skinless chicken cutlets
2 cloves garlic, minced
¾ cup chicken broth
¼ cup *French's®* Dijon Mustard
2 cups fresh spinach, washed and torn
⅓ cup heavy cream
1 package (9 ounces) fresh linguine pasta, cooked

1. Heat *1 tablespoon oil* in large nonstick skillet over high heat. Add chicken; cook 5 minutes or until browned on both sides. Add garlic; cook and stir just until golden.

2. Combine broth and mustard. Pour over chicken. Heat to boiling. Reduce heat to medium-low. Cook 5 minutes or until chicken is no longer pink in center.

3. Stir in spinach and cream. Heat to boiling. Cook 1 minute or until slightly thickened and spinach wilts. Serve over linguine. Garnish with minced parsley, if desired.

Makes 4 servings

Stir-Fried Pasta with Chicken 'n' Vegetables

Prep Time: 5 minutes
Cook Time: 15 minutes

6 ounces angel hair pasta, broken in thirds (about 3 cups)
¼ cup *Frank's® RedHot®* Cayenne Pepper Sauce
3 tablespoons soy sauce
2 teaspoons cornstarch
1 tablespoon sugar
½ teaspoon garlic powder
1 pound boneless skinless chicken, cut in ¾-inch cubes
1 package (16 ounces) frozen stir-fry vegetables

1. Cook pasta in boiling water until just tender. Drain. Combine *Frank's RedHot* Sauce, *¼ cup water,* soy sauce, cornstarch, sugar and garlic powder in small bowl; set aside.

2. Heat *1 tablespoon oil* in large nonstick skillet over high heat. Stir-fry chicken 3 minutes. Add vegetables; stir-fry 3 minutes or until crisp-tender. Add *Frank's RedHot* Sauce mixture. Heat to boiling. Reduce heat to medium-low. Cook, stirring, 1 to 2 minutes or until sauce is thickened.

3. Stir pasta into skillet; toss to coat evenly. Serve hot.

Makes 4 servings

Sesame Peanut Noodles with Green Onions

1 tablespoon peanut or vegetable oil
1 teaspoon finely chopped garlic
¼ cup SKIPPY® Peanut Butter
1 teaspoon soy sauce
2¼ cups water
1 package LIPTON® Noodles & Sauce—Chicken Flavor
½ cup sliced green onions
2 tablespoons sesame seeds, toasted (optional)

In medium saucepan, heat oil and cook garlic over medium heat 30 seconds. Stir in peanut butter and soy sauce; cook until melted. Add water and bring to a boil. Stir in noodles & sauce—chicken flavor, then simmer, stirring frequently, 10 minutes or until noodles are tender. Stir in green onions and 1 tablespoon sesame seeds. To serve, sprinkle with remaining 1 tablespoon sesame seeds. *Makes about 4 servings*

Penne with Eggplant and Turkey Sausage

1 pound Italian turkey sausage, cut into 1-inch pieces
1 medium eggplant, cut into ½-inch cubes
3 cups prepared chunky vegetable spaghetti sauce
12 ounces penne pasta, cooked according to package directions
4 ounces Asiago cheese, grated

1. In large nonstick skillet, over medium heat, sauté turkey sausage and eggplant 12 to 15 minutes or until sausage is no longer pink and eggplant is soft and lightly browned. Add spaghetti sauce to turkey mixture and simmer 3 minutes or until heated throughout.

2. To serve, spoon sauce over penne and top with cheese.

Makes 8 servings

Favorite recipe from **National Turkey Federation**

∽ QUICK TIP ∽

When purchasing eggplant, look for a firm eggplant that is heavy for its size, with tight glossy, deeply-colored skin. The stem should be bright green. Dull skin and rust-colored spots are a sign of old age. Refrigerate unwashed eggplant in a plastic bag for up to 5 days.

Tri-Color Pasta

Prep Time: 5 minutes
Cook Time: 10 minutes

1 package (16 ounces) tri-color pasta*
2 cups BIRDS EYE® frozen Green Peas
2 plum tomatoes, chopped *or* 1 red bell pepper, chopped
1 cup shredded mozzarella cheese
⅓ cup prepared pesto sauce or to taste

Or, substitute 1 bag (16 ounces) frozen tortellini.

• In large saucepan, cook pasta according to package directions. Add peas during last 5 minutes; drain in colander. Rinse under cold water to cool.

• In large bowl, combine pasta, peas, tomatoes and cheese. Stir in pesto.
Makes 4 servings

QUICK TIP

Plum tomatoes, sometimes called Italian tomatoes, are small and oval in shape. In season, tomatoes should be plump and heavy with a vibrant color and a pleasant aroma. They should be firm but not hard. A soft tomato will either be watery or overripe. Avoid those that are cracked or have soft spots.

Pesto Turkey & Pasta

Prep Time: 10 minutes
Cook Time: 20 minutes

¼ cup milk
1 tablespoon margarine or butter
1 (4.7-ounce) package PASTA RONI® Chicken & Broccoli Flavor with Linguine
1 pound boneless, skinless turkey or chicken breasts, cut into thin strips
1 medium red or green bell pepper, sliced
½ medium onion, chopped
½ cup prepared pesto sauce
¼ cup pine nuts or chopped walnuts, toasted
Grated Parmesan cheese (optional)

1. In large saucepan, bring 1½ cups water, milk and margarine to a boil. Stir in pasta and Special Seasonings. Reduce heat to medium. Gently boil 1 minute.

2. Add turkey, bell pepper and onion. Return to a boil. Gently boil 8 to 9 minutes or until pasta is tender and turkey is no longer pink inside, stirring occasionally.

3. Stir in pesto. Let stand 3 to 5 minutes before serving. Sprinkle with nuts and cheese, if desired.
Makes 4 servings

Tip: To make your own pesto, blend 2 cups fresh parsley or basil, 2 cloves garlic and ⅓ cup walnuts in a blender or food processor. Slowly add ½ cup olive oil and ¼ cup Parmesan cheese.

Easy Pasta Primavera

Prep Time: 15 minutes
Cook Time: 20 minutes

**3 cups (8 ounces) rotini,
  uncooked**
2 cups water
**1 package (16 ounces) frozen
  vegetable blend**
**¾ pound (12 ounces) VELVEETA
  LIGHT® Pasteurized Prepared
  Cheese Product, cut up**
2 tablespoons reduced fat milk
**¼ teaspoon each garlic powder
  and pepper**

1. Bring pasta and water to boil in
saucepan; simmer 10 minutes or until
pasta is tender.

2. Add vegetables, Velveeta Light,
milk and seasonings. Stir until Velveeta
Light is melted and mixture is thoroughly
heated.   *Makes 4 to 6 servings*

Manhattan Turkey
à la King

Prep Time: 7 minutes
Cook Time: 20 minutes

8 ounces wide egg noodles
**1 pound boneless turkey or
  chicken, cut into strips**
1 tablespoon vegetable oil
**1 can (14½ ounces) DEL MONTE®
  Diced Tomatoes with Garlic
  and Onions**
**1 can (10¾ ounces) condensed
  cream of celery soup**
1 medium onion, chopped
2 stalks celery, sliced
1 cup sliced mushrooms

1. Cook noodles according to
package directions; drain. In large
skillet, brown turkey in oil over
medium-high heat. Season with salt
and pepper, if desired.

2. Add remaining ingredients, except
noodles. Cover and cook over
medium heat 5 minutes.

3. Remove cover; cook 5 minutes or
until thickened, stirring occasionally.
Serve over hot noodles. Garnish with
chopped parsley, if desired.
        Makes 6 servings

Hint: Cook pasta ahead; rinse and
drain. Cover and refrigerate. Just
before serving, heat in microwave or
dip in boiling water.

Mediterranean Orzo with Pesto

1 package (16 ounces) BARILLA® Orzo
1 container (about 7 ounces) prepared pesto sauce
½ cup (2 ounces) grated Parmesan cheese
1 teaspoon red pepper flakes
1 jar (6 ounces) marinated artichoke hearts, drained, cut in half
¾ cup pitted kalamata olives *or* 1 can (6 ounces drained weight) whole pitted small ripe olives, drained
Salt and pepper

1. Cook orzo according to package directions; drain.

2. Combine orzo, pesto sauce, cheese and red pepper flakes in large bowl. Stir in artichokes, olives and salt and pepper to taste. Serve immediately.

Makes 8 to 10 servings

∾ QUICK TIP ∾

The word orzo is Italian for barley, but it actually refers to a small, rice-shaped pasta. It is often used in soups and as a substitute for rice.

Bow Tie Pasta and Sausage

6 sun-dried tomato halves, cut into ¼-inch strips
1 pound HILLSHIRE FARM® Smoked Sausage, cut into bite-size pieces
6 tablespoons olive oil
½ cup coarsely chopped onion
1 clove garlic, finely chopped
¼ teaspoon red pepper flakes (optional)
1 pound uncooked bow tie pasta
1 package (10 ounces) frozen lima beans
2 tablespoons coarsely chopped Italian parsley (optional)
Freshly ground black pepper

Place tomatoes in small bowl. Add ½ cup boiling water to bowl; let stand until softened, about 20 minutes. Meanwhile, cook Smoked Sausage in medium nonstick skillet over medium-high heat until browned. Remove sausage; set aside. Add oil and onion to skillet. Cook until onion becomes golden, about 5 minutes. Add sausage, garlic and red pepper flakes, if desired.

Cook pasta in large saucepan 2 minutes. Stir in lima beans. Cook, stirring occasionally, about 8 minutes. Drain; return pasta and beans to saucepan.

Add tomatoes and soaking water, parsley, if desired, and sausage to pasta and beans in saucepan. Heat over medium heat, stirring until blended, about 1 minute. Sprinkle with black pepper and serve.

Makes 6 servings

Mediterranean Orzo with Pesto

ON THE SIDE

Oven-Roasted Vegetables

1½ **pounds assorted cut-up fresh vegetables***
3 **tablespoons I CAN'T BELIEVE IT'S NOT BUTTER!® Spread, melted**
2 **cloves garlic, finely chopped**
1 **tablespoon chopped fresh oregano leaves or**
1 **teaspoon dried oregano leaves, crushed**
Salt and ground black pepper to taste

*Use any combination of the following: zucchini, red, green or yellow bell peppers, Spanish or red onions, white or portobello mushrooms and carrots.

Preheat oven to 450°F.

In bottom of broiler pan, without rack, combine all ingredients. Roast 20 minutes or until vegetables are tender, stirring once.

Makes 4 servings

Skillet Zucchini

Prep Time: 10 minutes
Cook Time: 8 minutes

3 **cups sliced zucchini**
2½ **cups sliced mushrooms**
1 **medium red bell pepper, cut into strips**
2 **tablespoons olive or vegetable oil**
1 **cup KRAFT® 100% Grated Parmesan Cheese**

• Cook and stir zucchini, mushrooms and pepper in oil over medium-high heat 5 to 6 minutes or until vegetables are crisp-tender.

• Remove from heat. Sprinkle with Parmesan cheese; cover. Let stand 2 minutes before serving.

Makes 4 servings

Oven-Roasted Vegetables

Rosemary Garlic Potatoes

Prep Time: 15 minutes
Cook Time: 25 minutes
Total Time: 40 minutes

4 large red skin potatoes, cut into wedges (about 2 pounds)
1½ teaspoons dried rosemary leaves
1 teaspoon garlic powder
2 tablespoons FLEISCHMANN'S® Original Margarine, melted

1. Toss potatoes with rosemary and garlic in large bowl; arrange on lightly greased baking pan in single layer. Drizzle with melted margarine.

2. Broil 4 inches from heat source for 25 to 30 minutes or until tender, turning potatoes over once.

Makes 4 servings

Acorn Squash with Maple-Butter

2 medium acorn squash
LAWRY'S® Seasoned Salt
3 tablespoons margarine or butter
3 tablespoons maple syrup
¼ teaspoon ground nutmeg

Microwave Directions
Pierce squash in several places. Microwave whole squash on HIGH 10 to 12 minutes; let stand 2 minutes and cut in half crosswise. Slice off ends, if necessary so halves will be level. Remove seeds and sprinkle cavities with Seasoned Salt. In 13×9×2-inch glass baking dish, place squash cut side up. Divide butter and maple syrup among squash halves. Cover with plastic wrap, venting one corner. Microwave on HIGH 30 seconds longer. Sprinkle with Seasoned Salt and nutmeg; let squash stand 3 minutes before serving. *Makes 4 servings*

Conventional Directions: Pierce squash in several places. Bake in 375°F. oven 1 to 1½ hours until tender. Cut in half crosswise. Slice off ends, if necessary so halves will be level. Remove seeds and sprinkle with Seasoned Salt. On baking dish, place squash cut side up. Divide margarine and maple syrup among halves. Bake 5 minutes. Sprinkle with Seasoned Salt and nutmeg.

Substitution: Butternut squash can replace acorn squash.

Serving Suggestion: Serve in quarters or sliced ½-inch thick.

Rosemary Garlic Potatoes

Oriental Fried Rice

Prep Time: 5 minutes
Cook Time: 10 minutes

1 tablespoon vegetable oil
1 egg, beaten
1 box (10 ounces) BIRDS EYE®
   frozen Oriental Style or
   Stir-Fry Style Vegetables
2 cups cooked rice*
2 tablespoons soy sauce

*Need cooked rice in a hurry? Prepare instant white or brown rice, then proceed with recipe.

• Heat 1 teaspoon oil in large skillet over high heat. Add egg; let spread in pan to form flat pancake shape.

• Cook 30 seconds. Turn egg over (egg pancake may break apart); cook 30 seconds more. Remove from skillet; cut into thin strips.

• Remove seasoning pouch from vegetables. Add remaining 2 teaspoons oil to skillet; stir in vegetables and rice.

• Reduce heat to medium-high; cover and cook 5 minutes, stirring twice.

• Add contents of seasoning pouch, soy sauce and cooked egg to skillet; mix well.

• Cook, uncovered, 2 minutes or until heated through.   *Makes 2 servings*

Festive Sweet Potato Combo

Prep Time: 10 minutes
Cook Time: 38 minutes

2 cans (16 ounces each) sweet
   potatoes, drained
1⅓ cups *French's® Taste Toppers™*
   French Fried Onions, divided
1 large apple, sliced into thin
   wedges
2 cans (8 ounces each) crushed
   pineapple, undrained
3 tablespoons packed light
   brown sugar
¾ teaspoon ground cinnamon

Preheat oven to 375°F. Grease 2-quart shallow baking dish. Layer sweet potatoes, ⅔ cup **Taste Toppers** and half of the apple wedges in prepared baking dish.

Stir together pineapple with liquid, sugar and cinnamon in medium bowl. Spoon pineapple mixture over sweet potato mixture. Arrange remaining apple wedges over pineapple layer.

Cover; bake 35 minutes or until heated through. Uncover; sprinkle with remaining ⅔ cup **Taste Toppers**. Bake 3 minutes or until **Taste Toppers** are golden.   *Makes 6 servings*

Oriental Fried Rice

Vegetable Parmesan Bake

**1 envelope LIPTON® RECIPE
    SECRETS® Garlic Mushroom
    Soup Mix**
¼ cup grated Parmesan cheese
**1 large baking potato, cut into
    ¼-inch-thick slices**
**1 medium zucchini, diagonally
    cut into ¼-inch-thick slices**
**1 large tomato, cut into
    ¼-inch-thick slices**
**1 tablespoon margarine or
    butter, cut into small pieces**

1. Preheat oven to 375°F. In small bowl, combine soup mix and Parmesan cheese; set aside.

2. In shallow 1-quart casserole sprayed with nonstick cooking spray, arrange potato slices, overlapping slightly. Sprinkle with ⅓ of the soup mixture. Top with zucchini slices, overlapping slightly. Sprinkle with ⅓ of the soup mixture. Top with tomato slices, overlapping slightly. Sprinkle with remaining soup mixture. Top with margarine.

3. Bake, covered, 40 minutes. Remove cover and bake an additional 10 minutes or until vegetables are tender.   *Makes 4 servings*

Recipe Tip: For delicious tomatoes any time of the year, store them on your kitchen counter out of direct sunlight, as sunlight can change their color without ripening the flavor or texture. And never store them in the refrigerator, as this can spoil their flavor and texture.

Balsamic Roasted Potatoes

Prep Time: 10 minutes
Cook Time: 30 minutes

⅓ cup balsamic salad dressing
¼ cup LA CHOY® Soy Sauce
**1 to 1½ pounds small red
    potatoes, cut into quarters**
**1 green bell pepper, cut into
    1-inch pieces**
**1 medium onion, cut into
    quarters**

In small bowl, combine salad dressing and soy sauce; set aside. In 17×11-inch baking dish, combine potatoes, pepper and onion; add soy sauce mixture and toss to coat. Bake at 450°F for 25 to 30 minutes or until potatoes are tender.

Makes 6 servings

QUICK TIP

To chop peppers easily, first cut them in half and remove the seeds. Then place the halves, skin side down, on a cutting board and cut them into smaller pieces.

Vegetable Parmesan Bake

Honey Nut Squash

2 acorn squash (about 6 ounces
    each)
¼ cup honey
2 tablespoons butter or
    margarine, melted
2 tablespoons chopped walnuts
2 tablespoons raisins
2 teaspoons Worcestershire
    sauce

Cut acorn squash lengthwise into
halves; do not remove seeds. Place
cut sides up in baking pan or on
baking sheet. Bake at 400°F 30 to
45 minutes or until soft. Remove
seeds and fibers.

Combine honey, butter, walnuts,
raisins and Worcestershire sauce;
spoon into squash. Bake 5 to
10 minutes more or until lightly glazed.
Makes 4 servings

Microwave Directions: Cut acorn
squash lengthwise into halves and
remove seeds. Microwave according
to manufacturer's directions.
Combine honey, butter, walnuts,
raisins and Worcestershire sauce;
spoon into squash. Microwave at
HIGH (100%) 30 seconds or until
thoroughly heated and lightly glazed.

Favorite recipe from **National Honey Board**

Double Cheddar Bacon Mashed Potatoes

Prep Time: 10 minutes
Cook Time: 20 minutes

2 pounds all-purpose potatoes,
    peeled and sliced
1 jar (16 ounces) RAGÚ® Cheese
    Creations!® Double Cheddar
    Sauce, heated
5 slices bacon, crisp-cooked and
    crumbled (about ¼ cup)
1 teaspoon salt

1. In 3-quart saucepan, cover
potatoes with water. Bring to a boil
over high heat. Reduce heat to low
and simmer uncovered 15 minutes or
until potatoes are very tender; drain.
Return potatoes to saucepan. Mash
potatoes.

2. Stir Ragú Cheese Creations! Sauce
into mashed potatoes. Stir in bacon
and salt. *Makes 6 servings*

Tip: Stir in ¼ cup chopped green
onions for an extra flavor boost.

✎ QUICK TIP ✎

It's important to heat the sauce (or
any liquid) before adding it to the
mashed potatoes; otherwise, the
potatoes will become gluey.

Honey Nut Squash

Garden Pasta Salad

1½ cups snow peas
1½ cups sliced carrots
1½ cups cauliflower florets
8 ounces BARILLA® Campanelle,
cooked according to
package directions
½ cup honey dijon salad dressing

1. Cook snow peas, carrots and cauliflower in boiling water 3 minutes; drain.

2. Combine cooked campanelle and vegetables in large bowl.

3. Just before serving, add salad dressing; toss lightly.

Makes 6 to 8 servings

Tip: Serve with additional dressing on the side.

Creamed Spinach

Prep Time: 5 minutes
Cook Time: 10 minutes

2 cups milk
1 package KNORR® Recipe
Classics™ Leek Soup, Dip
and Recipe Mix
1 bag (16 ounces) frozen
chopped spinach
⅛ teaspoon ground nutmeg

• In medium saucepan, combine milk and recipe mix. Bring to a boil over medium heat.

• Add spinach and nutmeg, stirring frequently. Bring to a boil over high heat. Reduce heat to low and simmer, stirring frequently, 5 minutes.

Makes 6 servings

Simply Green Beans

1 pound fresh green beans, ends
removed and cut in half
crosswise
1 tablespoon butter, melted
3 tablespoons coarsely grated
Romano cheese
¼ to ½ teaspoon LAWRY'S®
Seasoned Pepper
¼ teaspoon LAWRY'S® Garlic
Powder with Parsley

In large saucepan, bring 2 quarts of water to a boil over medium-high heat; add beans. After water has returned to a boil, cook beans 4 minutes. Drain; rinse under cold water. In medium skillet, heat butter. Add green beans and cook over medium-high heat 3 minutes or until tender. Add remaining ingredients; toss well. Serve hot.

Makes 4 servings

Serving Suggestion: Great accompaniment to roast chicken or fresh fish fillets.

Microwave Directions: In microwave-safe shallow dish, place green beans and ¼ cup water. Cover with plastic wrap, venting one corner. Microwave on HIGH 14 to 16 minutes, stirring after 7 minutes; drain. Add butter, Seasoned Pepper and Garlic Powder with Parsley. Stir; let stand covered 1 minute. Sprinkle with cheese.

Garden Pasta Salad

Savory Skillet Broccoli

Prep Time: 5 minutes
Cook Time: 10 minutes

1 tablespoon olive or vegetable oil
6 cups fresh broccoli florets or 1 pound green beans, trimmed
1 envelope LIPTON® RECIPE SECRETS® Golden Onion Soup Mix*
1½ cups water

*Also terrific with LIPTON® RECIPE SECRETS® Onion Mushroom Soup Mix.

1. In 12-inch skillet, heat oil over medium-high heat and cook broccoli, stirring occasionally, 2 minutes.

2. Stir in soup mix blended with water. Bring to a boil over high heat.

3. Reduce heat to medium-low and simmer covered 6 minutes or until broccoli is tender.

Makes 4 servings

Sautéed Peppers and Onions

2 medium-size red onions, peeled
1 red bell pepper
1 green bell pepper
1 tablespoon vegetable oil
2 tablespoons KIKKOMAN® Teriyaki Marinade & Sauce

Cut onions and peppers into ¼-inch-wide strips. Heat oil in large skillet over high heat. Add onions and peppers; cook and stir 2 minutes. Drizzle teriyaki sauce evenly over vegetables; toss to combine. Remove from heat.   *Makes 6 to 8 servings*

Broiled Ranch Mushrooms

1 pound medium mushrooms
1 packet (1 ounce) HIDDEN VALLEY® Original Ranch® Salad Dressing & Recipe Mix
¼ cup vegetable oil
¼ cup water
1 tablespoon balsamic vinegar

Place mushrooms in a gallon-size plastic food storage bag. Whisk together salad dressing & recipe mix, oil, water and vinegar. Pour over mushrooms; seal bag and marinate in refrigerator for 30 minutes, turning occasionally. Place mushrooms on a broiling rack. Broil 4 inches from heat for about 8 minutes or until tender.

Makes 4 to 6 servings

SIMPLY DELICIOUS

DESSERTS

Lemon-Blueberry Pie Cups

Prep Time: *15 minutes*
Refrigerate Time: *2¼ hours*

6 vanilla wafer cookies
¾ cup canned blueberry pie filling
1 cup boiling water
1 package (4-serving size) JELL-O® Brand Lemon Flavor Gelatin
¾ cup cold water
½ tub (8 ounces) COOL WHIP® Whipped Topping, thawed

PLACE one vanilla wafer on bottom of each of 6 dessert cups. Top each wafer with 2 tablespoons pie filling. Set aside.

STIR boiling water into gelatin in large bowl at least 2 minutes until completely dissolved.

STIR in cold water. Refrigerate 10 to 15 minutes or until mixture is slightly thickened (consistency of unbeaten egg whites). Stir in ½ of the whipped topping until well blended. Spoon over pie filling in cups.

REFRIGERATE 2 hours or until firm. Garnish with remaining whipped topping, if desired.

Makes 6 servings

Great Substitutes: Try using cherry or pineapple pie filling instead of the blueberry pie filling.

Best of the Season: Garnish each serving with fresh berries, if desired.

Lemon-Blueberry Pie Cups

Chocolate Nut Bars

Prep Time: 10 minutes
Bake Time: 33 to 38 minutes

1¾ cups graham cracker crumbs
½ cup butter or margarine,
  melted
1 (14-ounce) can EAGLE® BRAND
  Sweetened Condensed Milk
  (NOT evaporated milk)
2 cups (12 ounces) semi-sweet
  chocolate chips, divided
1 teaspoon vanilla extract
1 cup chopped nuts

1. Preheat oven to 375°F. Combine crumbs and butter; press firmly on bottom of 13×9-inch baking pan. Bake 8 minutes. Reduce oven temperature to 350°F.

2. In small saucepan, melt Eagle Brand with 1 cup chocolate chips and vanilla. Spread chocolate mixture over prepared crust. Top with remaining 1 cup chocolate chips, then nuts; press down firmly.

3. Bake 25 to 30 minutes. Cool. Chill if desired. Cut into bars. Store loosely covered at room temperature.
Makes 24 to 36 bars

Baked Ginger Pears

Prep Time: 15 minutes
Bake Time: 25 minutes

2 cans (16 ounces each) pear
  halves in extra light syrup,
  undrained
1½ cups cold fat free milk
1 package (4-serving size)
  JELL-O® Vanilla Flavor Fat
  Free Sugar Free Instant
  Reduced Calorie Pudding
  & Pie Filling
¾ teaspoon ground cinnamon,
  divided
½ teaspoon ground ginger,
  divided
1 cup POST® GRAPE-NUTS® Cereal

HEAT oven to 350°F.

DRAIN pears, reserving ½ cup syrup. Slice pears. Place in 8-inch square baking dish.

POUR reserved syrup and milk into medium bowl. Add pudding mix, ½ teaspoon cinnamon and ¼ teaspoon ginger. Beat with wire whisk 2 minutes or until well blended. Pour over pears.

MIX cereal, remaining cinnamon and ginger in small bowl. Spray lightly with no stick cooking spray; toss to coat. Sprinkle over pudding mixture.

BAKE 25 minutes or until heated through. Serve warm.
Makes 8 servings

Great Substitute: Used canned peaches instead of canned pears.

Chocolate Nut Bars

Banana Caramel Spice Pie

Prep Time: 10 minutes
Chill Time: 4 hours

1 large ripe banana, sliced
1 (6-ounce) READY CRUST®
   Shortbread Pie Crust
2 cups cold milk
2 (4-serving-size) packages
   white chocolate or vanilla
   flavor instant pudding & pie
   filling
½ teaspoon ground cinnamon
1 (8-ounce) tub whipped
   topping, thawed
   Caramel ice cream topping

1. Place banana slices in bottom of crust.

2. Pour milk into large bowl. Add pudding mixes and cinnamon. Beat with wire whisk 1 minute. Gently stir in whipped topping. Spoon into crust.

3. Refrigerate 4 hours or until set. Serve with caramel topping.
Makes 8 servings

Brownie Berry Parfaits

Prep Time: 10 minutes

1 box (10 ounces) BIRDS EYE®
   frozen Raspberries*
4 large prepared brownies, cut
   into cubes
1 pint vanilla or chocolate ice
   cream
4 tablespoons chocolate syrup
2 tablespoons chopped walnuts

*Or, substitute Birds Eye® frozen Strawberries.

• Thaw raspberries according to package directions.

• Divide half the brownie cubes among four parfait glasses. Top with half the ice cream and raspberries. Repeat layers with remaining brownie cubes, ice cream and raspberries.

• Drizzle chocolate syrup over each parfait; sprinkle with walnuts.
Makes 4 servings

❧ QUICK TIP ❧

Brownies will be easier (and less messy) to cut if you freeze them for a short time first, just until firm.

Banana Caramel Spice Pie

Dump Cake

1 (20-ounce) can crushed pineapple with juice, undrained
1 (21-ounce) can cherry pie filling
1 package DUNCAN HINES® Moist Deluxe® Yellow Cake Mix
1 cup chopped pecans or walnuts
½ cup (1 stick) butter or margarine, cut into thin slices

Preheat oven to 350°F. Grease 13×9-inch pan.

Dump pineapple with juice into pan. Spread evenly. Dump in pie filling. Spread evenly. Sprinkle cake mix evenly over cherry layer. Sprinkle pecans over cake mix. Dot with butter. Bake 50 minutes or until top is lightly browned. Serve warm or at room temperature.

Makes 12 to 16 servings

Tip: You can use DUNCAN HINES® Moist Deluxe® Pineapple Supreme Cake Mix in place of Moist Deluxe® Yellow Cake Mix.

Easy Cookie Bars

Prep Time: 15 minutes
Bake Time: 30 minutes

½ cup (1 stick) butter *or* margarine, melted
1½ cups HONEY MAID® Graham Cracker Crumbs
1⅓ cups (3½ ounces) BAKER'S® ANGEL FLAKE® Coconut
1 cup BAKER'S® Semi-Sweet Chocolate Chunks
1 cup chopped nuts
1 can (14 ounces) sweetened condensed milk

HEAT oven to 350°F. Line 13×9-inch baking pan with foil; grease foil.

MIX butter and graham cracker crumbs in medium bowl. Press into prepared pan. Sprinkle with coconut, chocolate chunks and nuts. Pour condensed milk over top.

BAKE 25 to 30 minutes or until golden brown. Cool in pan on wire rack. Lift out of pan onto cutting board.

Makes 3 dozen

Tip: For 13×9-inch glass baking dish, bake at 325°F.

Special Extra: Melt ½ cup BAKER'S Semi-Sweet Chocolate Chunks as directed on package. Drizzle over top of bars.

Oatmeal Stack Cake

1 package (14 ounces) oatmeal cookies
¼ cup milk
1 tub (8 ounces) COOL WHIP® Whipped Topping, thawed
Fresh strawberries
Fresh mint leaves

CRUSH 1 cookie; set aside.

BRUSH remaining cookies with milk; spread each with whipped topping, using about 2 cups. (Refrigerate remaining whipped topping.) Stack in groups of 4 or 5. Lay stacks together, end to end, on large sheet of plastic wrap to form a roll; press stacks together lightly to secure. Wrap in the plastic wrap.

REFRIGERATE 6 to 8 hours or freeze 4 hours. Just before serving, unwrap roll; place on platter. Spread remaining whipped topping over roll. Sprinkle with reserved crushed cookie. Garnish with strawberries and mint leaves. To serve, cut cake diagonally into slices.   *Makes 10 servings*

Baked Apples

2 tablespoons sugar
2 tablespoons GRANDMA'S® Molasses
2 tablespoons raisins, chopped
2 tablespoons walnuts, chopped
6 apples, cored

Heat oven to 350°F. In medium bowl, combine sugar, molasses, raisins and walnuts. Fill apple cavities with molasses mixture. Place in 13×9-inch baking dish. Pour ½ cup hot water over the apples and bake 25 minutes or until soft.   *Makes 6 servings*

Warm Chocolate Strawberry Cake Tarts

Prep and Cook Time: 12 minutes

⅓ package (10¾ ounces) frozen pound cake, thawed
¼ cup plus 2 tablespoons prepared hot fudge sauce
2 tablespoons Amaretto or coffee liqueur (optional)
6 to 8 strawberries, sliced
3 tablespoons strawberry jam, melted
Additional prepared hot fudge sauce
Toasted slivered almonds
Vanilla ice cream

1. Cut cake into 4 equal slices. Place 2 slices together, long sides touching, on cutting board. Cut out circle from cake slices using 3-inch cutter. Repeat with remaining 2 slices to make 2 circles total.

2. Combine ¼ cup plus 2 tablespoons hot fudge sauce and liqueur, if desired, in glass measure.

3. Microwave at HIGH 30 seconds. Divide sauce evenly between 2 plates; tilt plates to swirl sauce to rim. Arrange cake circles over sauce. Arrange strawberries in ovelapping circles over cake. Brush strawberries with jam.

4. Microwave tarts, one at a time, at HIGH 30 seconds or until warm. Top with additional hot fudge sauce and slivered almonds. Serve with ice cream.   *Makes 2 servings*

Oatmeal Stack Cake

Chocolate Peanut Butter Cups

**1 package DUNCAN HINES®
Moist Deluxe® Swiss
Chocolate Cake Mix**
**1 container DUNCAN HINES®
Creamy Home-Style Classic
Vanilla Frosting**
½ cup creamy peanut butter
**15 miniature peanut butter cup
candies, wrappers removed,
cut in half vertically**

1. Preheat oven to 350°F. Place
30 (2½-inch) paper liners in muffin
cups.

2. Prepare, bake and cool cupcakes
following package directions for basic
recipe.

3. Combine vanilla frosting and
peanut butter in medium bowl. Stir
until smooth. Frost one cupcake.
Decorate with peanut butter cup
candy, cut-side down. Repeat with
remaining cupcakes and candies.
Makes 30 servings

Tip: You may substitute DUNCAN
HINES® Moist Deluxe® Devil's Food,
Dark Chocolate Fudge or Butter
Recipe Fudge Cake Mix flavors for
Swiss Chocolate Cake Mix.

Strawberry Shortcakes

Prep Time: 6 minutes
Bake Time: 12 minutes

6 tablespoons sugar, divided
**1 pint sliced strawberries
(about 2 cups)**
**2⅓ cups BISQUICK® Original
Baking Mix**
½ cup milk
**3 tablespoons butter *or*
margarine, melted**
**1 tub (8 ounces) COOL WHIP®
Whipped Topping, thawed**

HEAT oven to 425°F.

MIX 3 tablespoons sugar into
strawberries; set aside. Stir baking mix,
milk, butter and 3 tablespoons sugar
in bowl until soft dough forms. Drop by
6 spoonfuls onto ungreased cookie
sheet.

BAKE 10 to 12 minutes or until golden
brown. Split warm shortcakes; fill and
top with strawberries and whipped
topping. *Makes 6 servings*

Special Extra: For a more decadent
dessert, try adding 1 cup BAKER'S®
Semi-Sweet Chocolate Chunks into
the baking mix and proceed as
directed above. Drizzle with your
favorite chocolate sauce.

Chocolate Peanut Butter Cups

Easy Chocolate Cheesecake

Prep Time: 10 minutes
Bake Time: 40 minutes
Refrigerate Time: 3 hours

2 packages (8 ounces each) PHILADELPHIA® Cream Cheese, softened
½ cup sugar
½ teaspoon vanilla
2 eggs
4 squares BAKER'S® Semi-Sweet Baking Chocolate, melted, cooled slightly
1 OREO® Pie Crust (9 inch)

HEAT oven to 350°F.

BEAT cream cheese, sugar and vanilla in large bowl with electric mixer on medium speed until well blended. Beat in eggs until blended. Stir in melted chocolate. Pour into crust.

BAKE 40 minutes or until center is almost set. Cool completely on wire rack. Refrigerate 3 hours or overnight.
Makes 8 servings

To soften cream cheese in the microwave: Place 1 completely unwrapped 8-ounce package of cream cheese in a microwavable bowl. Microwave on HIGH for 15 seconds. Add 15 seconds for each additional package of cream cheese.

Bananas Foster

6 tablespoons I CAN'T BELIEVE IT'S NOT BUTTER!® Spread
3 tablespoons firmly packed brown sugar
4 medium ripe bananas, sliced diagonally
2 tablespoons dark rum or brandy (optional)
Vanilla ice cream

In 12-inch skillet, bring I Can't Believe It's Not Butter! Spread, brown sugar and bananas to a boil. Cook 2 minutes, stirring gently. Carefully add rum to center of pan and cook 15 seconds. Serve hot banana mixture over scoops of ice cream and top, if desired, with sweetened whipped cream.
Makes 4 servings

Note: Recipe can be halved.

Strawberry Honey Parfaits

1⅓ cups low-fat sour cream
¼ cup honey
2 teaspoons lime juice or 1 teaspoon grated lime peel
4 cups strawberries
¼ cup coarsely chopped amaretti (Italian crunchy almond cookies) or biscotti
4 mint sprigs (optional)

Mix sour cream, honey and lime juice in medium bowl until well blended. Reserve 4 strawberries for garnish; coarsely chop remaining strawberries, about 3½ cups. Gently fold chopped strawberries into cream mixture; spoon into 4 (10- to 12-ounce) goblets or serving bowls. Sprinkle with 1 tablespoon cookie crumbs. Garnish with strawberries and mint sprigs, if desired. Serve immediately or refrigerate up to 6 hours.
Makes 4 servings

⌒ ACKNOWLEDGMENTS ⌒

The publishers would like to thank the companies and organizations listed below for the use of their recipes and photographs in this publication.

Barilla America, Inc.

Birds Eye®

Bob Evans®

ConAgra Grocery Products Company

Del Monte Corporation

Dole Food Company, Inc.

Duncan Hines® and Moist Deluxe® are registered trademarks of Aurora Foods Inc.

Eagle® Brand

Egg Beaters®

Fleischmann's® Original Spread

The Golden Grain Company®

Grandma's® is a registered trademark of Mott's, Inc.

Hillshire Farm®

The HV Company

Keebler® Company

Kikkoman International Inc.

Kraft Foods Holdings

Lawry's® Foods, Inc.

National Honey Board

National Turkey Federation

Perdue Farms Incorporated

Reckitt Benckiser

Riviana Foods Inc.

The J.M. Smucker Company

Tyson Foods, Inc.

Unilever Bestfoods North America

Index